Student Workbook

for

Toseland and Rivas

An Introduction to Group Work Practice

Fourth Edition

prepared by

Rich Furman
Colorado State University

Allyn and Bacon
Boston   London   Toronto   Sydney   Tokyo   Singapore

Contents

ABOUT THE AUTHOR

Dr. Rich Furman serves as an assistant professor in the School of Social Work at Colorado State University, Fort Collins, CO. He has taught practices courses in both the BSW and MSW programs, including *Generalist Practice: Small Client Systems* (MSW program), *Advanced Generalist Practice with Individuals (*MSW program*), Advanced Generalist Practice with Groups and Families* (MSW program), *Introduction to Social Work Research* (MSW program), *Generalist Practice with Large Client Systems* (MSW advanced standing program), *Introduction to Generalist Practice with Small Groups* (BSW program), *Seminar in Child Welfare Practice with Hispanics and Native Americans* (BSW program) and *Senior Seminar* (BSW program).

Dr. Furman has worked in various roles in social work practice and education for fifteen years. He is the founding director of Children's Outreach Services Programs, Resources for Human Development, Philadelphia, PA. This innovative wrap-around program provides home and school-based services to children and adolescents with emotional and mental health disorders. He also founded and directed an early intervention program for the same agency. He has been a clinical social work conducting individual, group and family therapy with adults, children and families in the various communities. He was the supervisor of group therapy for a substance abuse program in the Puerto Rican community in Philadelphia.

Dr. Furman was also previously the Director of the Youth Work Certificate Program at Community College of Philadelphia, and a member of the faculty in the department of Behavioral Health and Human Services.

Dr. Furman has published numerous articles on social work ethics, managed care, youth services, social work education, friendship, and poetry in social work. His work has or will soon appear in journals such as Journal of Social Work Education, Social Work Education, International Social Work, The Journal of Sociology and Social Welfare, Australian Social Work, Advances in Social Work as well as many others.

He is also an internationally published poet whose work has appeared in nearly one hundred literary journals. His manuscript of poems, *The Trotting Race of Time*, chronicles his insight into social movements and life in Central America.

ACKNOWLEDGMENTS

I would first like to extend great appreciation and thanks to the faculty of the School of Social Work at Colorado State University for their warmth, caring and support.

I would specifically like to thank two colleagues for their support and encouragement. To Dr. Eleanor Downey, who has always made herself available to me for dialogue about teaching. Her skill-based approach to helping students learn to become social workers has helped me refine my teaching style. Dr. "D" is a master teacher who I learn from constantly.

Also, to Dr. Robert L Jackson, currently associate professor of social work at University of Washington-Tacoma. Bob helped me understand what it means to be a productive scholar and quality teacher, and a good person, at the same time. Cheers Bob, you're a dear friend.

Perhaps I am most indebt to the students I have taught over the years. Their willingness to take risks has helped me refine many of the exercises in this workbook.

As always, my appreciation to my soul mate and wife, Jill Furman, who not only has provided me with immeasurable emotional support, but is a fine editor as well.

Love and gratitude to Maya and Rebecca, for knowing just the right moment to give their dad a hug and a kiss, and when to leave the working bear alone.

Thanks to the authors of the text this workbook accompanies, Dr. Ronald W. Toseland and Dr. Robert F. Rivas. I learn new things from them each time I read their fine text.

Finally, thanks to Patricia Quinlin of Allyn and Bacon, for according me the honor of putting together this book. Pat's availability to me during this project made it enjoyable. She is a delight to work with. Thanks also to Annemarie Kennedy, also of Allyn and Bacon, for her help with the project.

Lastly, to all my friends, who provide me with the strength and resiliency to strive. Peace, hope and dreams.

INTRODUCTION

Teaching is humbling experience that provides constant opportunity for learning and personal growth. Over the years, students have bravely taught what they need from me to help facilitate their learning and growth. This has been especially true for teaching courses on group work. Students have shown me how I must create experiences that help them practice and own the concepts and skills that they read about and that are discussed in class. Practice cannot be learned solely through listening to lectures and reading. Students have taught me that the best theories or approaches that I may teach them are only valuable to the degree that *they* may put them into practice.

Over the years, I have also come to understand the true importance of the social work axiom "the professional use of self." It is through the vehicle of the social work practitioner that our interventions with clients are enacted. In a very real sense, we are our own set of tools. As with the tools of any trade or profession, they must be kept in good working order. Social work students therefore are called upon to work on themselves, understand their vulnerabilities and weaknesses, as well as maximize their already copious strengths. This workbook seeks to be one aid in this journey. My educational philosophy, and the underlying principle that guided the creation of this workbook, is based upon the notion of praxis, the application of theory and knowledge into action through the person of a reflective practitioner.

The exercises in this workbook have been constructed with several ideals in mind. First and most importantly, they are meant to amplify the wonderful text that it accompanies. Students will find the Drs. Toseland and Rivas' teaching clear, insightful, practical, and worthy. As you will notice, this workbook begins on chapter three, and corresponds directly to chapters three through fourteen in their text. The workbook includes in-class exercises, exercises for writing and reflection, case studies, and projects that will help students "own" the concepts and skills they have learned.

The exercises in the workbook are designed to help group work instructors empower students to put what they have learned into action. Each semester, students tell me that the most valuable aspect of their group work class had been the hands experiences. For instructors less inclined towards in-class group experiences, there are case examples and exercises that are to be conducted outside of class.

It is my hope that different instructors will chose to use the exercise in various ways. I encourage instructors to modify learning experiences and exercises to meet their personal styles and the needs of their students. While the exercises may be valuable in and of themselves, they also can be invaluable ways of stimulating class discussion.

Students of this workbook will find some of the exercises personally challenging. This workbook is not meant to help you memorize concepts for true and false exams: it has been designed to help prepare you for real practice, which often is emotionally demanding work. As I say to my group class at the beginning of each semester, your learning will be directly proportionate to the work you put into it. This is especially true in regard to sections titled "for writing and personal reflection." Spending the time to work through these exercises can help you develop the ability to think critically and reflectively about your practice. In my experience, this skill is one of the most important for social workers to possess.

I hope you find going through this workbook educational. I also hope you have fun with it. I hope you take your learning seriously, but remember: the definition of enlightenment, is to lighten up. Enjoying your learning is simultaneously a gift, and a choice.

CHAPTER THREE- UNDERSTADNING GROUP DYNAMICS

Exercise 3.1-Communication and interactional patterns: Sending and receiving messages

Objective- Students will develop an understanding of how messages can become distorted in their transmission between sender and receiver.

In class exercise- One of the most important ways group leaders facilitate the creation of positive group dynamics is by facilitating healthy patterns of communication. Distortions in communication between the sender and the receiver of the message are common. In this exercise, students work together in triads. Each student will take turns playing the role of the client, the group worker, and an observer. The client and the worker are to have a dialogue that could occur in a group. The goal is for the student who is role-playing the worker to reflect back to the client, as best they can, the meaning of what the client has said. You may use the three scenarios listed below or invent your own.

Scenario #1
A treatment group for Latino men in an outpatient substance abuse program. Jose just learned that he lost his job, and has been feeling like drinking.

Scenario #2
A psychoeducational group for new mothers. Linda, a 19-year-old single mother, is discussing her fears about losing the best years of her life to a new baby, and the shame of having these feelings.

Scenario #3
A community group for neighbors to discuss their feelings about a new group home for homeless, mentally ill men that is being planned for the community. Mac is a 50-year-old man who has lived on the block his whole life. He is angry the group is being built on his street, but has some empathy towards the men.

For writing and reflection

1. In the role of the worker, what was it like for you when you were not able to fully understand your client?

2. In the role of the client, what was it like when you were not fully understood by the worker?

3. What behaviors did you witness as the observer that facilitated clear communication?

4. What behaviors did you witness as the observer that seemed to lead to communication problems?

5. Reflecting upon this experience, what behaviors or skills would you like to continue to develop?

6. List a few action steps that you will use to develop these new behaviors.

Exercise 3.2-Cohesion

Objective- Students will develop an increased understanding of the factors that lead to group cohesion.

For written reflection-Group cohesion is essential for optimal group functioning. People often affiliate with groups to meet social needs that are not being met in other areas of their lives. Facilitating proper group cohesion can lead to better outcomes, as people become more invested in the group experience. Often called the "all in the same boat" phenomenon, group leaders must constantly work towards building cohesion. Spend some time addressing the following reflection questions related to group cohesion.

1. Think about group experiences you have had where the group members exhibited a high degree of cohesion. What was the group like? What were the behaviors of the group leader that helped you feel close to and part of the group? What were the behaviors of your fellow group members that contributed to this feeling?

2. Think about group experiences you have had where group members exhibited a low degree of cohesion. What was the group like? What were the behaviors of the group leader which lead to poor cohesion? What were the behaviors of your fellow group members that contributed to this feeling?

3. Review the list of factors that effect group cohesion on page 80 of your text, as well as the practice principles on the same page. Imagine for a moment that you were the leader of the above group that you noted had poor cohesion. Keeping these factors and principles in mind, how would you change that group?

Exercise 3.3- Norms

Objective- Students will begin to think through the process of developing positive norms in groups.

Norms are overt and covert expectations and beliefs about how members of groups should act. Overt norms are those that have been discussed, while covert norms are unspoken rules that guide behavior. Some covert rules are helpful (i.e. not interrupting when someone is speaking, or being kind to others), while other covert norms can lead to problems in group dynamics (i.e. nobody shares deep or risky feelings, or nobody says anything that is not met with the approval of a powerful member).

To alter them, covert norms must be identified and discussed. By identifying and exposing these norms to the "light of day" (making them explicit to members of the group), covert norms often lose their power. Group members can be encouraged to explore these norms and consciously replace them with overt norms that are more helpful. By involving group members in this process, they are helped to feel in control of their group, thus increasing cohesion.

In class exercise- In pairs or small groups (or, if the instructor does not break you into groups, use this exercise for writing and reflection) discuss the covert and overt norms in your classes. What norms are helpful and what norms are not helpful? What would be some more helpful norms which could be substituted that would lead to improved group dynamics?

For reflection and writing: What group norms do you find most troublesome? How do these norms affect your behavior in groups? What norm would you like to see in place of these norms?

Exercise 3.4- Understanding behavior in the context of group stages

Since many of the behaviors of group leadership are predicated on the stage of development of the group, it is important to understand the various stages of group development, and what is normative during each stage. In the beginning stages, most groups are concerned with planning, organizing, and establishing cohesion and positive norms. During the middle phases, the group should be focused on its main work, whether this is the completion of a specific task or growth and support. The ending stage should be characterized by the completion and evaluation of group efforts. This may entail completing tasks or dealing with separation.

For reflection and writing: List examples of behavior that may run counter to the normative group behavior for each stage. How might these behaviors negatively impact the functioning of a group?

1. Beginning stage

2. Middle stage

3. Ending stage

For class discussion- Discuss the issues that each class member came up with. How would you deal with these problems if they encountered them in task or treatment groups? (This can also be done as a writing and reflection exercise).

Exercise 3.5- Group dynamics case example

Jim is a social worker at a community mental health program in a large city. He provides individual and group therapy in an outpatient forensic program. Most of Jim's clients have had significant histories of committing violent crimes. The majority of them have spent time in prison. The purpose of the program is to help his clients cope with their mental health and substance abuse issues which are contributing factors to their committing violent crimes.

One of the groups that Jim leads is for female offenders with histories of violent behavior. The group consists of ten members. Jim prefers his groups to have eight members, yet even though these clients are mandated by the legal system to attend all treatment requirements, including group, rarely do all members show up. The group started five sessions ago, and is open ended, although actual turnover in the group is anticipated to be relatively low. On most days, between five and seven women show up to the group. A core of four have attended each of the first sessions.

Jim starts each week by asking the women how they are doing, and if anyone would like to share what happened during their week. He believes that this helps the members of his group take ownership for their own treatment. For the past two weeks, members have not spoken in response to his invitation. He got the sense that Carol wanted to share, but that something stopped her. He remembers a few weeks prior when Carol was sharing about her incest, she immediately stopped sharing in the middle of her story. When she stopped, she averted her eyes from one side of the group. One of the members of the group appeared to be staring at her very intently, with a smile on her face that Jim perceived as odd.

Jim decided to conduct a check in round to see how the members were doing, to get them to share at least some information, and to break what he perceived to be tension in the room. Jim decided to start his round so that it ended on Jill, the women who was staring so intently at Carol while she spoke of her incest. Jim asked the members to rate how they were feeling and doing this past week on a scale from one to ten, ten being fantastic, one being terrible. The majority of the women in the group reported numbers between 3 and 6. Tomika, an African American women who suffers from bipolar disorder, reported a 2. Jill reported a nine. When the round stopped, Jim asked Tomika if she would like to share about why she scored her week so low. Scanning the group to gauge the responses of the members, Jim noticed that several members were looking at Jill, and that they were shifting uncomfortably in their chairs. Tomika seemed to look at Jill before deciding if she wanted to share or not. Jill immediately said, "Well, I don't think we should talk about people who had bad weeks. I mean, I had a great week, and I think I want to talk about it. Why do we always have to focus on the garbage? I mean, I had a messed up week in some ways, but that's life, why should we talk about it, you know." Jim thanked Jill for speaking up, and told her while he understood her feelings about discussing negative events, and that it was sometimes very painful, he believed that sometimes people needed to get things off their chest, or get feedback about things so they can change them. Betsy, a young African American women with a history of being sexually abused, started to laugh uncontrollably. She said that she had the funniest thing happen to her during the week, and something Jill said had reminded her of this. She started to get up from her chair and quickly started to do an impression of a friend. As Carol began to cry Jill started to get up and leave the group. Jim asked for everyone to sit down and relax for a few minutes. He said that he felt that the group was going through a hard period, and that it was important to figure out what was going on. He first asked the group if they would take a few minutes to sit in silence and try to "get ourselves together." Jill and Betsy sat down and the group slipped into momentary silence.

For writing and reflection

After having read chapter three in your text and having completed the previous exercises on group dynamics, write your sense about the group dynamics of the preceding case example. Answer the following questions to help guide you in your assessment.

1. What can you tell about the nature of the communication and interaction patterns in the group?

2. Describe your sense of the group's cohesion.

3. Describe the norms of the group.

4. Describe the rules of the group

5. Discuss various roles different group members play.

6. How would you describe the culture of the group?

7. What would it be like to lead such a group?

8. How might the group leader intervene in altering some of these dynamics?

CHAPTER FOUR- LEADERSHIP

Exercise 4.1- Assessing leadership skills

Objective- Students will develop a sense of their own strengths and weaknesses in relationship to their leadership abilities.

Leadership self assessment exercise

Leadership skills are behaviors and activities that help a group achieve its aims and individual group members to achieve their goals. While leadership skills may at times be overemphasized as factors contributing to the outcome of a group, they are still important. Students and experienced group leaders alike should continuously evaluate their leadership skills and work towards improvement. Some of these "skills" are actually personal attributes that we can work on developing. These include sense of humor, trustworthiness, authenticity, enthusiasm, flexibility and humility.

For writing and reflection or discussion in pairs

1. To what degree are you comfortable in the position of leader? What about being in the position of leader is most difficult for you?

2. Which of the characteristics of good leaders do you feel are your strengths?

3. How do these strengths help you as a leader?

4. Which of the characteristic of good leaders do you believe you need to develop more fully?

5. How do these areas of growth currently get in your way as a group leader?

6. Create a plan for developing these new skills.

Exercise 4. 2- Focus

Objective- Students will develop the ability to keep a group focused, while balancing the need to allow group members autonomy and self determination.

Group leaders must strike a balance between direction and democracy; they must avoid being overly controlling of the groups interaction yet focus group members on productive work. Jacobs (2001) addresses several important skills pertaining to focus: Establishing focus, maintaining focus, deepening focus, and shifting focus.

In class exercise- In groups of four or five, take turns being the leader for ten minutes. The leader will choose a topic that they would like to discuss. The leaders will want to consciously practice each of the focusing skills. Each leader should make sure they clearly establish the focus, maintain focus on the topic throughout, deepen the focus to a level that moves beyond superficiality, and for practice shift the focus to another topic or ending.

For writing and reflection

1. What behaviors did you find helpful in regard to each area of focusing?

2. What was the hardest thing to do? Why?

3. Did you feel uncomfortable shifting the focus? If so, what made this difficult?

4. Did you feel uncomfortable deepening the focus? If so, what does this mean for you?

5. Based upon this exercise, which skills would you like to improve? How can you go about making these improvements?

Exercise 4.3 Scanning

Objective- Students will develop the ability to pay attention to the individual members' and the group simultaneously.

Scanning is a group skill that is as important as it is difficult to master. When one scans, they simultaneously pay attention to the group member who is speaking as well as the rest of the group members. Scanning is a vital skill. If a group leader focuses only on an individual and not the group as a whole, they will soon find that they are the center of attention, and all communication will soon go through them. Lack of scanning often leads to low levels of group member participation.

In class exercise- Break into groups of five. There should be an additional person for each group to serve as an observer/consultant. Each member will take turns being the group leader. For 5-10 minutes, the group leader will practice scanning while group members conduct a discussion. The goal of the exercise is for the leader to find a way of paying attention to the group member who is talking, as well as each member of the group. The consultant will gently remind the leader to "scan" if they begin to pay too much attention to individual members.

For writing and reflection

1. What was it like to scan the group?

2. In what way was it difficult?

3. Discuss ways you can improve your ability to scan?

Exercise 4.4- Coleadership

Objective- To develop a personal understanding of the benefits and potential pitfalls of coleadership.

Leading a group with another social worker or helping professional can be both helpful and difficult. The following exercise is designed to help you understand some of the advantages and difficulties of coleadership.

In class exercise- In pairs, students will colead a group for ten minutes. The group should consist of five to eight students who will serve as clients. For the purpose of this group, the other students should role play members of a drug and alcohol, inpatient treatment group. The group members will be asked to discuss issues related to their most recent relapse. The group leader's job is to help facilitate discussion. Normally, coleaders should do considerable planning and discuss potential issues before they lead a group (see figure 4.7 in your text). For the purpose of this assignment however, the leaders will go into the group cold. The coleaders should try to support their coleader and help facilitate the discussion.

For in class discussion

1. What were the difficulties of coleading the group with someone else?

2. What were the advantages in coleading the group?

3. Based upon this experience, what issues would you have liked to discuses with your coleader prior to leading this group?

For writing and reflection

1. What was it like for you when your coleader did something you disagreed with? Were you able to accept and support them? Did your verbal or non verbal behavior suggest disagreement? If so, how?

2. Did you feel supported by your coleader? Did they do anything that made you feel less supported? If so, what?

3. How may your own personal issues related to power and control impact your ability to colead a group with others?

4. What do you feel are your strengths related to coleading groups?

5. What skills do you feel you need to continue to develop in order to be an effective coleader?

6. List and discuss several steps you will take to improve your coleadership skills.

CHAPTER FIVE- LEADERSHIP AND DIVERSITY

Exercise 5.1- Understanding our cultural identity

Objective- Students will develop an increased sense of their own cultural identity.

By learning to understand their own cultural identity, social workers develop a sense of how cultural factors impact our behavior. This is especially important for group leaders who often lead groups with culturally diverse members. The questions below are designed to be written exercises. They may also be discussed in dyads, small groups, or with the entire class.

1. Describe your cultural and ethnic origin and identification?

2. In what ways is your culture important to you?

3. What are the key values of your culture? How might these values differ from other cultures?

4. How might these differences in values lead to conflicts with others?

5. How does your cultural background influence your behavior in groups?

6. Describe a time when you have felt different, or like an outsider. What was it like? How was your behavior different than in other situations?

7. How does your gender affect your behavior in groups? How does it affect your behavior towards those of the same and different gender?

8. What religious or spiritual issues affect your behavior in groups?

9. List and discuss a few ways that you can become more in-touch with your cultural background.

Exercise 5.2- Exploring our biases

Objective- Students will explore their biases and prejudices in working with those who are culturally different from themselves.

Most of us, whether we admit it or not, have internalized prejudiced beliefs. It is nearly impossible to have grown up in a society that is inundated with sexism, racism, classism, anti-Semitism, and homophobia to not have been influenced by these ideologies and behaviors. Exploring our biases and prejudices is one of the most painful things we can do, but one of the most liberating as well. When we recognize the influence of these often subtle beliefs, we can work to assure they do not impact our group leadership. To deny possessing these thoughts, gives them power over our leadership style by robbing us of our most important tool, or self awareness.

Writing and reflection- Since these are often difficult issues to address, complete them in a place where you feel safe. If you do not wish to keep the answers in this workbook, you may write them on a separate piece of paper, and if you wish, destroy it when you are done.

1. Think of the different ethnic groups in your community. What have you come to believe about them that may not be true?

2. Do you have any automatic thoughts or beliefs about certain ethnic or cultural groups in your community that come to mind when you are in their presence?

3. Are you uncomfortable around certain groups of people? What feelings do you have around them?

4. How is your behavior different around members of different ethnic or cultural groups?

5. Do you have any beliefs about men or women that may be overly generalized or untrue?

6. Are you comfortable around people who are gay, bisexual or transgender? What beliefs do you have about people of these groups?

7. Are there any groups with whom you may be uncomfortable working? How might this impact your social work practice?

Optional Exercise 5.3- Releasing our shame

There is an expression that we are only "as ashamed as our secrets." As we know from working with clients, when they express things that they are ashamed of and receive acceptance and validation, they are able to face their demons and make changes. The same is true for our prejudices. Expressing them to a safe person can help reduce our shame and the impact of these beliefs. As Martin Luther King said, "the truth shall set you free."

With a person who you feel is safe, discuss your answers to the previous questions. If this is done as an in-class exercise, make sure that all participants know that their job is to listen, support and accept. This is also a good exercise for practicing empathic listening.

For writing and reflection

1. What did you learn from this experience?

2. In what way might this change your beliefs or behavior?

3. What other beliefs do you need to let go of?

Exercise 5.4- Exploring differences and commonalities

Objective- To increase student's ability to see people holistically. To help develop the ability to place cultural influences within the context of the individual differences and universal commonalities.

Furman (2002) developed a model for understanding the individual based upon social constructionism. Social constructionism allows for the integration of three crucial domains of human consciousness and behavior: that which pertains to the individual, that which pertains to all people, and that which pertains to specific groups and cultures. For example, one could know that in traditional Guatemalan culture, birth control is typically perceived as being against the will of God. Conscious attempts at limiting family size are seen as meddling with the divine. The practitioner only looking at culture would assume that this culturally ascribed belief would *cause* a client to be highly resistant to birth control measures.

However, the social constructionist would suggest that cultural manifestations exist only in how they are interpreted by the individual. For instance, a particular woman might view this socio/religious doctrine as applying only to abortion and not to contraception. She may feel the weight of the values and norms that she learned from her socio/religious context, but may make an individual decision to act differently based upon her own personal free will.

The model, depicted as table 1 on the following page, is a graphic representation of this perspective.

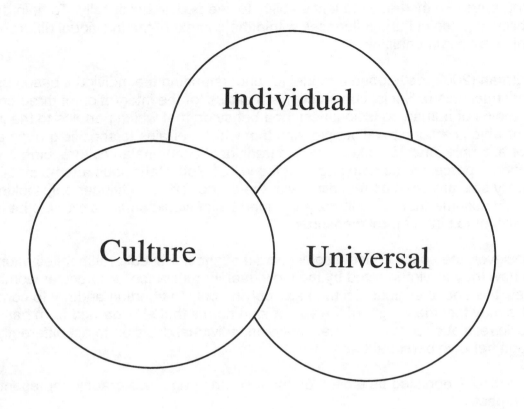

Table 1

In class exercise-Take turns leading small groups of 5-8 in class. For 10 minutes, lead a discussion from one of the topic listed below, or choose your own topic. If the topics is controversial, the leaders will want to make clear to the group that the purpose of their discussion is to help understand each other's perspective, not to agree or disagree. The leader will want to facilitate a discussion about how individuals have developed their beliefs, including information from each of the three domains discussed above.

Potential topics for discussion- Discipline of children, disagreeing with one's parents, the roles of men and women in performing housework, parent's living with their adult children, the importance of education for education sake (not merely to obtain a career), or abortion (be careful with this controversial topic).

For discussion in dyads

With a partner, conduct a multicultural assessment of your partner in regard one of the above listed topics. For ten minutes, see if you can learn the distinct role that each domain has played in shaping their beliefs and behavior. Many find it useful to draw the three domains as they are depicted in the table above, and place information into each circle. You may find that many specific beliefs, emotions and behaviors overlap domains, thus illustrating the dynamic interaction of human behavior and learning.

For writing and reflection

1. What did you learn form this exercise?

2. How might what you have learned be useful in assessment?

3. How might what you have learned be useful in group work

CHAPTER SIX- PLANNING

Exercise 6.1- Assessing sponsorship and potential membership

Objective- Assessing agency sponsorship for groups and potential membership of groups are related issues. Students will learn to evaluate agency sponsorship as it impacts group membership.

For writing and reflection
For the purpose of this exercise, think of the social service agency that you know best. If you have yet to work in a social service agency, you may use your school of social work for this exercise.

1. What are the unmet needs of clients in this agency?

2. What type of group might help meet these needs?

3. Describe the fit between the mission of the agency and/or program and the type of group you are thinking of creating.

4. What resources do you need to start the group successfully?

5. Who can help you secure the needed recourses?

6. Who might be resistant to starting this group? Why might they be resistant?

7. How can you help this person become invested in the group?

8. Describe the clients who may be potential members of this group.

9. What would be a good way of describing your group to clients in order to help them become interested in attending?

Exercise 6.2- Establishing group purpose

Objective-Being clear about the purpose of a group is important. Lack of clarity about the purpose of a group can lead to confusion and resistance in group members.

Written exercise

Describe three ways you would establish purpose in each of the following situations.

Example #1- A school-based psychoeducational group for patents with elementary age children diagnosed with ADHD.

Example #2- A community-based task group with various constituencies gathering to discuss community perceptions about a proposed chemical plant in the neighborhood.

Example #3- An inpatient therapy group for battered women.

For in class practice

With a partner, practice the statements that you developed. Give each other feedback about your statements of purpose.

For writing and reflection (After you finish your statement's of purpose)

1. What did you like about your partners statements of purpose?

2. What would you change about your partner's statement of purpose?

3. What were the strengths of how your partner delivered their statements of purpose?

4. What would you like to incorporate about the way your partner delivered their statement of purpose? What would you change about your delivery?

5. Based upon the feedback you received from your partner, what would you change about your statement of purpose?

6. Based upon this feedback, what would you change about your delivery?

Exercise 6.3- Practice in planning

Objective- Students will develop the ability to plan various types of groups and develop the ability to work collaboratively in the planning process.

To practice the planning process, you will be developing groups that would have been helpful after the September 11th tragedy. Teams of four will design a group to work with the following client population. In your plan you will want to decide upon a structure for the group as a whole, as well as a detailed outline of the first session. In constructing the format, take into account all of the issues you have learned in the text about planning groups. You will obviously have to account for group size, length of session, number of sessions, type of group, format or medium, as well as many other factors. Space is provided below for developing your plan.

Each team will work on creating a group to serve the population highlighted below.

     a. Islamic or Middle Eastern students your campus

     b. School children whose parents died in the tragedy.

     c. Witnesses to the tragedy who now suffer from anxiety and stress.

     d. Social work professionals wanting to discuss what can be done about the tragedy.

1. Important issues to consider

2. Overall structure of plan

3. First session plan

4. Final session plan

CHAPTER SEVEN- THE GROUP BEGINS

Exercise 7.1- The purpose of communication

Objective- Students will become increasingly aware of the motivation for people's verbal and non-verbal communication.

For writing and reflection-While communication issues are addressed in chapter three, understanding communication is essential to beginning a group. People in groups communicate to meet important interpersonal concerns. In this sense, most communication can be understood as designed to meet some psychosocial need. In this exercise, you will explore examples of how people communicate to meet these needs. Please provide examples from your own practice or personal experience, times when you have exhibited or witnessed examples of the communication witnessed below. Provide both verbal and non-verbal examples that are indicative of attempts to meet each communication need.

1. People attempting to demonstrate understanding

        B. Verbal

        C. Non verbal

2. Attempts at understanding another's feelings towards you, or how they perceive you.

        B. Verbal

        C. Non Verbal

3. Attempts at persuading someone to meet one's needs

4. Verbal

5. Non Verbal

4. Attempts at gaining or maintaining power in communication

    B. Verbal

    C. Non Verbal

5. Attempts at defending oneself from others

    D. Verbal

    E. Non Verbal

6. Attempts at providing feedback to others

    F. Verbal

    G. Non Verbal

7. Attempts at making an impression on others

    B. Verbal

    C. Non Verbal

8. Attempts at developing or maintaining relationships

    B. Verbal

    C. Non Verbal

9. Attempts of group members at expressing cohesion and unity

    A. Verbal

    B. Non Verbal

Exercise 7.2- Opening a group

Objective- Students will develop the ability to open groups using a variety of skills.

In class exercise-In a group of 6-8 students, take turns opening a group. You may role play a treatment group for men who have been convicted of spousal abuse, or develop your own group. The main purpose of the suggested group is to help the men learn to control their behavior.

Use the following skills for opening the group. The purpose is to practice different ways of opening groups, and then assessing what worked and what did not. Remember, the group leader must give clear directions for what they want group members to do and discuss.

Dyads-Members break into pairs for introduction to explore their expectations. Dyads are useful ways of encouraging all members of a group to communicate and work. Since dyads consist of two people, they replicate comfortable and familiar communication patterns.

Round robins- A round occurs when each member of the group take a turn responding to requested information. The leader can ask members to provide a word that describes how they feel about participating in a group, a one to ten rating on how they comfortable they are, or any other pertinent information. Rounds are a quick and useful way of obtaining valuable information.

An exercise- Exercises can set the tone of action and participation in a group

Statement of purpose and goals- The leader opens the group by discussing the expectations, procedure and norms of the group.

Personal writing and reflection

1. Which of these openings seemed to work the best for you? Why?

2. Describe something that one of your fellow student's did that you would like to incorporate into you style?

Exercise 7. 3- Analysis of group beginning

Objective- Students will consider options of starting the first session of a treatment group by analyzing a case study and developing alternative strategies.

For writing and reflection-Read the case example in your text on page 216 in your text. In this case example, a worker develops a plan and conducts a first session with teenage boys. Consider the following questions.

1. What do you believe was the most effective way the worker conducted the session?

2. What would you like to have seen done differently?

3. What would be some alternative ways of opening the group?

4. What would you do differently if the group was for girls instead of boys?

5. What factors would you have to consider if the group was for Latino boys?

6. African American boys?

7. Asian boys?

8. What might the worker have done differently in regard to the issue of confidentiality? What are the ethical issues involved in this area

9. What questions about this example would you like answered? See if you can discuss these questions in class and/or think of possible responses.

CHAPTER EIGHT- ASSESMENT

Exercise 8.1- Assessment of group dynamics

Objective- To help students develop the ability to assess group dynamics

Group leaders frequently do not spend enough time assessing group dynamics. As with assessing other aspects of groups, assessing group dynamics is not a one time event. A good group leader continually pays attention to the key areas of group development.

In class exercise
Students are asked to volunteer for a one session group on a topic relevant to the members of the class. It should be a topic that is intense enough for some personal investment, yet does not delve into the realm of therapy (for example, students' plans for the future once they graduate is a good topic). Select a group of five to eight students. The instructor of the course or a student shall lead a discussion group around this topic. The rest of the class will form a larger circle outside the group for the purposes of observation.

Each student should pay attention to the four dimensions of group dynamics: Communication and interaction patterns, cohesion, social control mechanisms, including norms, roles and status; and group culture. It would be useful to review chapter three of your text before this exercise. Once the group is completed, discuss as a class what each person observed.

For personal writing and reflection

1. What were your general impressions of this group?

2. What did the leader do well?

3. What would you do differently if you had been the leader?

4. What group dynamics seemed to be helpful to the group process?

5. What group dynamics seemed to detract from the group process?

6. Describe the various roles of the different group members.

7. Based upon your initial assessment, what would you do with this group if it met for subsequent sessions?

Exercise 8.2- Assessing the environment

Objective- Students will develop the ability to utilize the environmental context of the group and group members. In order to help students think about the impact of the environment, students will conduct an environmental scan related to their own functioning.

Environmental context refers to the agency setting of the group, as well as the social context of clients' lives. For a variety of reasons, including an increased focus on individuals as the source of problems in the helping, many group leaders fail to assess and understand the environmental context of group member's behavior.

For writing and reflection

1. In what whys does your environment help you meet your goals?

2. In what ways does your environment hinder achieving your goals?

3. What are the most important resources in your community? How do you use these resources, and how might you utilize them better?

4. Think about the various interactions you have with social institutions (i.e. work, school, religious groups). How do these institutions help you meet your needs? How do they shape your behavior?

5. List your needs which are currently not being met. What types of social supports might help you meet these needs?

6. How might you better utilize the people in your life for support? Who would these people be?

7. Based upon your assessment above, develop an action plan to better meet your needs and develop your strengths through improved utilization of your environment.

Exercise 8.3- Assessing problem solving and coping

Objective- Students will draw connections between understanding their own coping and the ability to assess the coping of others.

Clients often come to groups in distress. When people are experiencing increased stress, they often do not cope as well as they normally do. It is important for group leaders to assess problem solving skills and coping strategies which clients have used previously.

Part one
In class exercise- In groups of five to eight students, a leader will assess students coping with stress. The leader will lead a discussion by starting with the following statement: Each of you have stated in the past that being a student can be very stressful. Sometimes we cope with stress well, and sometimes we do not. I am interested in those times when we cope with stress well. I would like us to talk about how we managed stress, specifically those times when we are doing a good job managing it. Who would like to start?

For writing and reflection- Answer the following questions individually after you have completed this exercise in class.

1. What did the leader do well?

2. What did you learn about coping?

3. What did you learn about groups from this exercise?

Part two

For writing and reflection- Conduct an assessment of your own coping mechanisms about the stress of school. Answer the following questions in as much detail as possible.

1. What are some indicators that tell you when you are feeling stress?

2. What changes in your life when you are feeling particularly stressed?

3. How do you relate to and treat people when you are feeling very stressed?

4. What coping mechanisms work for you when you are feeling very stressed?

5. What coping mechanisms help you managed your life?

6. Do you engage in any negative coping mechanisms or bad habits to reduce stress? Describe these behaviors and their impact?

7. How well are you dealing with your stress now? How does this compare to times when you are optimally handling your stress?

8. Devise a "treatment plan" for yourself. Based upon the assessment of your coping, what would you like to do differently?

Exercise 8.4- Self-anchored rating scales

Objective- By working to develop new self anchored rating scales, students will develop a new and useful assessment tool for helping individuals in groups assess and monitor their own behavior.

Self anchored rating scales are useful assessment tools. These rating scales help group members monitor behaviors they are attempting to change. In order to help group members learn to develop their own scales, it is useful to practice developing them for yourself.

In-class exercise- Figure 8.1 of your text provides you with a schema for a self-anchored rating scale. With a partner, develop two self-anchored rating scales for each other around behaviors that you struggle with (.i.e. procrastination, depression, anxiety, stress, burn out, ect.).

For writing and reflection

1. How might such scales actually be useful in your own life?

2. Understanding the nature of your own resistance can help you be more empathic to the resistance of clients. What would prevent you from utilizing these scales?

CHAPTER NINE- TREATMENT GROUPS: FOUNDATION METHODS

Exercise 9.1- Five intervention roles

Objective-Students will practice each of the main intervention roles. Students will become aware of which roles are most comfortable for them, and which one's they need to develop further.

Social workers have five intervention roles that they may utilize with clients in order to help them meet their treatment goals. Each of these roles represents a different set of skills that can be practiced and developed. These skills are: 1) Enabler, 2) Broker, 3 Mediator 4) Advocate, and 5) educator.

Part one
For personal writing and reflection- To help increase your insight, current skill level and comfort with each role, review page 275 of your text and answer the following questions.

1. Describe your experience with each of these roles in groups and other helping situations.

2. In which of these roles do you feel most comfortable and competent? Why?

3. In which of these roles do you feel least comfortable and competent? Why?

4. What skills do you need to develop in order to become more comfortable and competent in each of the roles?

5. List and discuss three things you can do to develop these skills.

Part two
In class activity- For this activity, students should divide into groups of five. You will pick a topic that is of interest to everyone in the group. For five minutes each, you will take turns being the leader. During your time as leader, you goal is to attempt to take each of these roles at least once. Try to see it as a game and assume each of the roles. Group members should not be too resistant and difficult during this exercise. Due to the degree of artificiality created by attempting to switch roles so quickly, the leader may not always be as sensitive as they otherwise would be. After the group is over, discuss the following questions as a group, as a class, or use the spaces for writing and reflection.

1. For each of the above roles, identify one member of your group who preformed a role well. Discuss how they preformed the role and what skills were involved.

2. Discuss any changes you would like to make as to how you preformed each role.

Exercise 9.2- Handling reluctance and resistance in treatment groups

Objective- Students will learn how to deal with reluctant and resistant clients by practicing to validate their feelings.

Many clients come to group with reluctance to participate. Some clients are mandated by the legal system, feel coerced by other service providers, or come to treatment to save relationships. Regardless of the degree of their resistance, workers must validate clients' often mixed feelings about participating in groups. Additionally, workers should try to uncover feeding and thoughts that underlie their behavior. Often, resistance can serve as a means of self protection.

In class exercise- In pairs, practice responding to the following behaviors or statements.

1) A 19 year old Puerto Rican client is mandated to drug and alcohol treatment as part of his sentence for dealing drugs. The client states " I am only here cause' my PO (probation officer) told me I have to come, but nobody can make me change anything."

2) In a group for battered women, a 32 year old woman tells the group that she is not going to talk about what her husband did to her. She says "I am here to listen and learn how to live my life, but I am not going to talk about what has happened to me."

3) An eight year old in a play therapy group for hyperactive boys sits with his arms crossed during the first three sessions, and does not say anything.

4) A 65 year old man in a support group for new residents of an assistant living situation states "I don't believe in this group therapy stuff. It will not make me healthy again, and it will not bring back my wife. What do you think you can really do for me?"

For writing and reflection- Since dealing with resistant and reluctant clients is often difficult, it is important to explore your own feelings and responses in regard to working with reluctant and resistant clients.

1. What is the most difficult thing about working with resistant and reluctant clients?

2. What are your biggest fears in working with reluctant clients?

3. In your responses to the scenarios above, what did you do well?

4. In your responses in the scenarios above, what would you like to have done differently?

Exercise 9.3- Exploring strengths- Mining for hidden strengths

Objective- Students will develop the ability to identify strengths in group members as means of helping them overcome difficulties.

Since members of treatment groups usually join to help them resolve specific problems, it is easy for group leaders to become overly focused on problems or deficits. However, a key principle of social work practice is that individuals will often overcome their problems and difficulties when they are helped to maximize their internal and external strengths and resources.

In class exercise- In dyads, conduct an interview of a classmate. The purpose of the interview is to discover as many of their strengths as possible. During the interview, you will want to look for general strengths, as well as strengths related to culture. Try to find as many positive things about the person as you can. Explore how each of these strengths have been used to fulfill their dreams and meet their challenges.

For writing and reflection

1. What did you learn about the person you interviewed that might not have been discovered if you had focused solely on their problems or issues?

2. How was the tone or quality of this interview different from interviews you have conducted in the past?

3. How have the person's strengths helped them overcome the dilemmas in their lives?

4. What strengths did you discover from that person's culture and cultural experience?

5. How might group work be different if the leader focused on strengths rather than problems or weaknesses?

6. How might this exercise impact your group work practice?

7. What skills does one need in order to work from a strengths perspective?

Exercise 9.4- Treatment group case example

Sally is a social worker for Children's Care Society an agency which provides residential treatment services to children and adolescents in community based group homes. Most of the children and teens who have been placed in the homes have emotional or behavioral problems that have proven to be too challenging for their parents to managed, or are children in the foster care system who cannot be maintained safely in traditionally foster care. Sally is responsible for individual, group and family therapy for five houses of adolescent girls. The group homes implement a milieu treatment approach, whereby para- professional residential treatment counselors implement treatment plans that Sally develops. Sally holds group sessions with each group of children twice a week. Each group varies in size, depending upon the number of residents in each house. The groups are open ended, yet many of the clients live in the home from six to twelve months. At times there is fluctuation in membership, as clients occasionally are hospitalized, run away, or are discharged to a more or less restrictive setting.

One house of girls has recently started to get out of control. The two girls who have a history of acting out behavior have involved several of the six other girls in leaving without permission, coming home late, and possibly drinking and using other drugs. The two girls are currently at risk of being placed in a more restrictive setting far from the city. During a recent session, Sally started a conversation about an event that happened the previous night. Four of the girls had left the group home after dinner, and did not return until three in the morning. Sally stated that the purpose of the group for that day would be to help the girls look at their behavior and see what the potential consequences would be, and to help them make choices. Joan and Kim, the two girls who were the primary leaders, both said that they did not have to talk about anything that they did not want to talk about, since Sally had told the group that they could set the agenda. Expressing empathy, Sally answered that there was merit to their argument, that the group was for them, and that they certainly could not be made to discuss anything they did not want to talk about. Sally also explained that the situation in the group home had escalated to a point that if changes did not occur, it was likely that they would be placed in more secure settings and would have far fewer choices given to them in the near future. Sally suggested that she would like to help prevent this from happening, and that she hoped the girls would make choices now that would preserve their right to make choices in the future. Sally said that it was impossible for her to make them stay in the group, and that it was merely her job to help them reach their goals. Sally pointed out to Kim that she had the stated goal of being a singer, and to Joan that she wanted to become a veterinarian. She posed a question to the group: How are your current choices going to affect your future goals? Two of the girls that were followers of Kim and Joan began to discuss their fears of the future, and worried how their behaviors might be affecting their lives. One discussed how her friends had told her that she was starting to change, and that this bothered her.

For writing and reflection

1. What might the worker do at this point to help Kim and Joan?

2. Which of the five social work roles might be useful for the worker to take at this point? Describe different roles that might be of value?

3. What kind of resistance and reluctance might the worker receive at this point, and how might they deal with it?

4. What type of planning might the worker do for the next session?

5. What type of activities or exercises might be useful?

CHAPTER 10- TREAMENT GROUPS: SPECIALIST METHODS

Exercise 10.1- Implementing plans

Objective- Students will practice implementing a plan for a treatment group, thereby practicing the process of converting plans into action.

Below is a plan written for a treatment group for stress. For this assignment, you will want to break into a group of 6-8 students, with the rest of the class serving as observers. Either the instructor or a student may serve as the group leader. The leader will want to enact this group plan to deal with stress. The members of the group should not role-play, but will be asked to be honest and real about what life events are causing them stress. The assigned leader should be given a week to prepare for leading the group.

5 minutes- Round: Names of members and current level of stress 1-10.

5 minutes- Mini lecture: The causes of stress.

10 minutes- Dyads: Discussion of personal stresses

10-15 minutes- Group discussion processing dyads: Focus on communalities and solutions.

15 minutes- Time permitting: Teach relaxation method.

5 minutes- Process and end.

Part one
For class discussion-After the exercise, discuss in class what worked well and potential areas for improvements, both in terms of the leader's behavior and the plan.

Part two

For writing and reflection- Create your own plan for a stress group. What would you do differently than the plan above? Write out your plan in the following space. Put it away for a day, and then critique it. By not critiquing your plan right away, you will give yourself the space to be more objective.

Exercise 10. 2- Interpersonal intervention: Applications to self

Objective- Students will work though a structured process of change so they may become more familiar with implementing change.

It is far easier to guide group members through a change process if you have worked through one yourself. When a client comments that change is hard and might not be possible, being intimately aware of the dynamics of working through change will help you address them in a less hypothetical or detached, clinical manner. This is not to say that you must self disclose what issues you have worked on in your own life, but having worked on change ourselves usually leads to a greater level of authenticity. Having worked through the process yourself, you will be able to remember what the steps felt like, and will have an easier time helping people through their resistance to change.

For writing and reflection- Pick one problem that you would like to change. The questions below will help guide you through the four steps of interpersonal change discussed in chapter 10:

1) Describe the nature of the problem.

2) Identify thoughts, feeling and actions that are associated with this problem.

3) Describe the connections between specific thoughts, feelings and behaviors.

4) Analyze the rationality of your thoughts and beliefs. How accurate are they? Do they help you in your life?

5) With what would you like to replace the behavior you are attempting to change?

6) Write down thoughts and beliefs that support your new behavior.

7) Develop a plan for following through on making the change.

Exercise 10.3- Metaphors and teaching techniques of cognitive change

Objective- Students will practice the process of helping group members work through cognitive change.

Several metaphors, stories and teaching tools are valuable means of helping clients understand the nature of changing their thoughts. In groups of between five and eight, take turns practicing using the tools discussed below. Practicing each of these techniques can help you incorporate them into your group leadership repertoire. Some of these techniques can be found in your text (see Table 10.1), while some of them are alternative options for you to consider and practice.

1. <u>Teaching story of the three vice presidents</u>- In this teaching story, I tell clients and students to imagine that on the same day, three vice presidents of different divisions of the same company were "downsized" (fired). I emphasize that their lives were basically all the same, married, the same number of children, the same number of dogs, ect. ect. However, the men each had very different emotionally and behavior responses to the event. One man became very depressed and attempted suicide. Another man was overjoyed and felt free. The third was sad, hurt and worried, but began his job hunt. I ask group members why the three men had different responses to the same event. They usually answer that they are different. I try to get them to explore specifically what makes them different in this moment. They usually are able to understand that it is their perceptions or the meaning they attach to the event that leads to their differing emotions. We then explore what their beliefs might have been. This usually leads to a wonderful discussion of the cognitive influence of behavior.

2. <u>Our brainwashing tapes</u>- For this teaching metaphor, group members are encouraged to think of some of their irrational or unproductive beliefs as a type of brainwashing. I like to use an actually tape to concretize the experience. I will say to them, for example, when you are feeling depressed, what messages does your tape play? I explain that sometimes it does not matter where or how they learned what their tapes say. Sometimes we cannot know. What is important, however, is that tapes can be recorded over. This allows for a discussion of what messages they would like to believe, and what messages would be healthy and productive.

3. <u>Use of gestalt empty chair technique</u> - In this exercise, group members use an empty chair to symbolize their symptom free selves. When they sit in this chair, I ask them to tell the group how they feel. Specifically, I ask them how they are seeing the world differently (perception and

belief). I also use the empty chair for group members to act as their own social workers. They are asked to switch back and forth between the client chair and the social worker chair. When in the role of the social worker, their job is to challenge the irrational and unhelpful beliefs that are keeping them stuck.

4. <u>Sculpting/ choreography-</u> See page 298 of your text.

5. <u>Rational role reversal-</u> In this exercise, the leader of the group role plays the client, and the client role plays the group leader. In this exercise, the leader, in the role of the client, must be very careful not to make the client feel mocked. The goal is for the client to develop insight into their behavior and thinking, and to act as their own therapist in the change process.

6. <u>Group feedback about irrationality-</u> In this exercise, the leader asks the group to give one of its member's direct feedback about their beliefs.

7. <u>Lending rationale beliefs-</u> The group leader gives cards to group members containing rationale and helpful beliefs. The cards can also be developed by group members for each other. The group leader tells the clients that these beliefs are on loan to them until they develop new, more helpful ones for themselves.

Exercise 10.4- Treatment group case example

Sue is a social worker who is also the paid staff member of a small program serving GLBT (Gay, lesbian, bisexual and transgender) members of the community. The purpose of the program is to help GLPT people meet their social needs and provide them with support. Sue runs several support groups for different constituents, as well as a therapy group. The therapy group is for depressed young GLBT people. The group is viewed as an adjunct to other forms of treatment, as most of the clients are also seeing Sue or other clinicians for individual therapy. Several of the clients are also taking anti depressants. The members of the group see it as being a valuable aid in overcoming their depression. Few mental health service providers in the very conservative community in which they live have much experience with openly GLBT people. During one particular session, Adam said that he was becoming increasingly depressed. Sue checked to see if he was thinking about, or planning on hurting himself. He stated that he was not thinking of harming himself, but was feeling as if life was hopeless. Adam is a junior at a local college, and recently came out to his parents. His parents, extremely conservative and members of a sect of a faith that views homosexuality as a sin, did not respond well. They kicked him out of the house and told him to not contact them as long as he "engaged in that lifestyle." Adam had been very close to his parents, and their rejection led him to question his value as a person. Adam wondered if his parents were right. He began to believe that he was indeed going to go to hell. He reasoned that since he could not deny his homosexuality, and thus would always be separated from his family, he would live in hell and die in hell. He became increasingly distant from old friends who accepted his homosexuality, as well as new friends in the GLBT community. Adam reported feeling different from many people in the group, since he is Mexican American and the other members are white. Other members of the group related to Adam. The leader asked the group if anyone would like to respond to Adam. Several expressed empathy and shared that while their situations might be different, each one of them felt a degree of isolation and shame that was impacting their lives and leading them to becoming depressed. Many of them also wondered out loud if they would ever feel less depressed, and wondered if treatment would ever help.

For writing and reflection-Placing yourself in the role of the worker, answer the following questions.

1. What cultural factors must be considered when developing treatment plans for members of this group?

2. What environmental interventions might be used to decrease the sense of isolation of the group members?

3. What within-group interventions might the worker use to decrease the isolation of its members?

4. What strategies might the worker use to change Adam's depression related to his beliefs, thoughts and feelings?

5. Develop a plan for a middle session for this group. Write the plan below.

6. Analyze the plan for potential problem areas

7. What other interventions might also be used to ameliorate some of the group members' depression?

CHAPTER ELEVEN-TASK GROUPS:FOUNDATION METHODS

Exercise 11.1- Dealing with conflict

Objective- To help students learn to increase their ability to tolerate the inevitable conflict that occurs in groups. By so doing, student will be better able to handle conflict in groups by being able to remain increasingly calm and poised.

Conflict is a nearly inevitable part of group work. In task groups, leaders must learn how to manage conflicts in order for tasks to be completed. Many people are uncomfortable dealing with conflict.

In-class exercise- This in-class exercise may also be done independently. The following questions may be written and reflected upon regarding your general reaction to conflict. Students will break into groups of five or six. They will simulate a task group meeting where there is a fair amount of conflict. In this exercise, the leader will not intervene, but should merely witness the conflict. It is important to note that normally, leaders must find ways of intervening during many conflicts. Students will take turns being leader and will tolerate conflict for five minutes.

For writing and reflection

1. Describe what was most difficult for you about being present during the group conflict?

2. What methods did you use to tolerate the conflict?

3. What can you do to increase your ability of tolerate conflict in the future?

Exercise 11.2- Responding to conflict

Objective- Now that students have increased their ability to tolerate conflict, they will increase their ability to manage it.

In-class exercise- In the same groups utilized for the previous exercise, students will take turns leading a task group in which there is conflict. This time, students will intervene to assure that the group will manage its conflicts. Make certain to review the steps for responding to conflict listed in your text book on pages 334 and 335.

For writing and reflection

1. What skills did you use well when helping resolve the conflict?

2. What was most difficult for you while attempting to resolve the conflict?

3. What might you do differently the next time a similar conflict arises?

4. What skills did fellow students use that you thought were effective?

Exercise 11.3- Implementing problem solving in task groups

Objective- Students will learn the problem solving approach as it is applied to task groups. Students will discover the advantages and disadvantages of using task groups verses individual decision making. Since the problem solving approach is an essential tool in social work practice, its utility goes far beyond the task group.

In-class exercise- Read pages 342-356 in your text book to reacquaint yourself with the problem solving approach as applied to task groups. In task groups of approximately six people, a leader will help the group work through the problem solving approach to the issue described below.

The director of your school of social work has just allocated $10,000 dollars to help students "create a greater sense of community." You have been asked by the director of the department to create a process for deciding how the funds will be used. In your task groups, develop this process.

For writing and reflection- After you finish the exercise, complete the following questions.

1. What worked well in this process?

2. What was difficult about this process?

3. How could the group have been conducted more effectively?

4. What would you say are the strengths of this process?

5. What are the weaknesses of this process?

6. What might be the advantages of this group process over coming up with a process on your own?

7. What would the disadvantages be?

Exercise 11.4- Task group case example

Robert is the director of a community based mental health agency. The agency provides intensive social work services to at risk children in their homes and schools. The goal of the program is to help patents and guardians, as well as teachers, maintain children with challenging behavioral and emotional problems in the least restrictive setting possible. Masters level social workers provide individual and family therapy, and bachelor level workers provide one on one intervention for several hours a day.

The program provides a desperately needed service in the urban area that it serves. It helps to reduce children's reliance on expensive inpatient and residential care. For these and other reasons, the program experienced tremendous growth during its first few years. The biggest problem the program had was hiring and training enough staff to meet its ever increasing demand. Sometimes during the third year of its life, the state contracted with managed mental health care organizations to manage mental health services in the city. At this point, things began to change rapidly for the program. Its rates were cut, and the amount of hours it was allowed to work with children decreased dramatically. Suddenly, a well-funded and solid program found itself having to come up with new challenges and constraints. Robert did his best to inform the staff of potential changes. He worked with his management team to find solutions to many of the programs problems. However, staff moral began to wane. The ambiguity and uncertainty led several experienced and valued staff to find new employment. Robert decided that he needed to involve staff more intimately in the decision making processes of the program.

*Expand case example to help it make sense in context of questions

For writing and reflection- Imagining you are Robert answer the following questions about how you would go about the meeting?

1. Where would you conduct these group meetings?

2. Who should be included in the meetings?

3. How large would the group meetings be?

4. What potential conflicts might arise? How might this conflict be dealt with?

5. How can members be specifically involved in the decision making process?

6. How might fact finding be facilitated?

7. What processes might be used to make effective decisions?

8. What are the potential political ramifications of these decisions?

9. How can work be monitored and evaluated?

CHAPTER TWELVE-TASK GROUPS: SPECILIZED METHODS

Exercise 12. 1- Brainstorming

Objective- To practice and develop skills in facilitating brainstorming.

Brainstorming is one of the most important methods of helping various types of task groups develop creative ideas and means of problem solving. During brainstorming energy is focused on creative thinking and generating ideas, not upon the evaluation of these ideas. Brainstorming thus helps groups think "outside the box."

In class exercise- After reading pages 360 through 364 in the text, students will divide into groups and practice brainstorming. One person will service as the leader during the exercise. The exercise can be repeated more than once so several students may lead. Suggested brainstorming topics are: Ways of improving your school of social work; ways of developing healthy friendships; things in the community that need to be improved; problems with welfare reform; or any other topic that you can think of. Remember the four rules for brainstorming: 1) freewheeling is welcome; 2) criticism is ruled out; 3) quantity is wanted; and 4) combining, rearranging, and improving ideas are encouraged. The leader should pay special attention to helping the group generate ideas, not evaluate them.

For writing and reflection

1. What went well during the brainstorming exercise(s)?

2. What would you do differently?

3. What do you perceive to be the value of using this technique?

Exercise 12. 2- Focus groups

Objective- Students will learn how to conduct a focus group

Focus groups are wonderful ways of collecting in-depth data about community needs, perceptions about agency functioning, and many other topics of interest in indirect or macro social work practice.

In class exercise- A team of two students are asked to volunteer to be the leaders a task group. They can conduct a focus group on any topic that might be appropriate to your school of social work at the time. They will prepare to conduct a task group the following week. They will make sure to plan a specific agenda, discuss methods for recruiting and screening students from the class and will thinking through methods of proper facilitating the group.

For writing and reflection- It is now your turn to analyze the data.

1. What were generalizations can be made from the data?

2. What can be learned from exceptions to patterns in the data?

3. What would your recommendations based upon the data?

Exercise 12.3- Task group skill assessment

Objective- To help students learn how to facilitate the assessment of group member skills in task groups.

In task groups, it is important to help individual members assess what they can contribute to the group. Since empowering individuals to take ownership for their assigned tasks is essential to successful task group facilitation, it is often useful to help individual group members assess their strengths related to the task.

In class exercise- In groups of five to eight, students will be asked to be members of the first session of a task group. The purpose of the group is to assess the resources in their community. In this exercise, the group leader will facilitate a group where the members assess their own skills in regard to this task. The leader will then help the group members discuss their strengths in regard to completing the task. It is important that the worker spend time drawing out and validating the strengths of the members. Members of task groups often have more skills and resources than they are aware of.

For writing and reflection

1. How well do you feel the group members assessed their own strengths?

2. What factors seem to lead to accurate self-assessment?

3. What might be the advantages of having group members assess their potential strengths, and choose actions based upon these strengths, verses having the leader assigning tasks?

Exercise 12. 4 Task group case example

Jose is an 18 year old young man who is caught in a conflict between himself, the school he attends, his wrap-around social worker (in the role of behavior specialist consultant), and the school district administration. Jose was referred for wrap-around services (community-based mental health services that provide treatment in the home, school or community) to help him succeed in his urban high school in the northeastern part of the United States. Jose started attending his school within the last few months. Prior to this, he lived in a residential treatment facility that had a self-contained school. Jose lived in residential treatment facilities for over 6 years. His mother, who raised him by herself, placed him due to his aggressive and often violent behavior. While in residential treatment, Jose was able to decrease the incidence of his aggressive behavior dramatically, although at times he was still aggressive towards peers and adults. He also carries the diagnosis of mild mental retardation.

When Jose turned 18, he left his placement and returned to the community. He found an inexpensive room near where his mother lived. Jose decided that he wanted to attend the local high school. Although he had not attended public school in over 5 years, he stated that he felt tired of going to "dummy schools" (private schools for children with developmental disabilities and partial hospitals). Still mandated to provide educational services for Jose, the school district placed him at his local high school in a special education class designed for students who are mildly intellectually disabled. While Jose is very happy being in the community high school, he is not happy with being placed in this class. Although he recognizes that he has "learning problems," he does not want to be in a class with adolescents who are mentally retarded, all of whom are lower functioning than himself.

After two weeks in class, Jose became verbally aggressive with the teacher's assistant and other teens. The school personnel began to see Jose not only as mentally retarded, but as having serious emotional and behavior problems as well. They have started to believe that Jose was inappropriate for their school. Jose, on the other hand, sees his aggression as being a function of his placement in a classroom that is not to his liking. School personnel told he and his mother not to come back to school until he had a one-on-one wrap-around worker with him for the entire school day. School personnel saw this as an intermediate step until a more appropriate school setting could be found by the school district administration.

A community team meeting, including Jose, his mother and his aunt, school personnel, a representative of the school district and the wrap-around social worker met to discuss the problem.

The conflict can be succinctly stated as follows. Jose is in conflict with the school, as he wants to return to school immediately, and does not want a one-on-one wrap-around worker with him full time. The school district does not want to pay for an approved private school placement, and thus is not in conflict with Jose, but with the school personnel. They also recognize that the school's sending Jose home for two weeks was a violation of his rights, and made them susceptible to litigation. School personnel did not want him back in school at all, but certainly not without full time intensive support. The wrap-around social worker was in conflict with the school; as his agency, and the funding source, would be willing to provide half-day services, but questioned the need for full-time interventions. Also, the social worker recognizes that it is the school's responsibility to provide an appropriate educational program for Jose, and that while wrap-around services can help Jose deal with his emotional and behavioral problems, it is the school and school district's responsibility to meet his educational needs.

For personal writing and reflection

1. What strategies would you use in the group to help negotiate a resolution of the conflict?

2. What potential difficulties do you see arising during this group?

3. What might be some tasks assigned to different group members in order to help resolve this situation?

4. What between-group tasks might the group leader do?

5. How would you evaluate the effectiveness of this group?

CHAPTER THIRTEEN-EVALUATION

Exercise 13.1- Observing accurately

Objective- Students will practice observation. While being able to accurately observe is an important skill in all group work practice, it is essential to the evaluation process.

Group exercise- In groups of five or six students, a leader will practice observing certain behaviors. Group members are to simulate a treatment group for persons suffering from low self-esteem. The worker should make note of the number of times group members engage in the following behaviors: sigh, interrupt, exhibit signs of discomfort, and exhibiting disinterest. Group members will also consciously keep track of how many times they exhibit each behavior, for the sake of comparison. After five minutes, the leader and group member should compare tallies. Each person in the group should take a turn in the role of the leader to practice their observation skills

For writing and reflection

1. In what ways was this exercise difficult?

2. What were the barriers to accurate observation?

3. What can you do to improve your ability to observe accurately?

Exercise 13.2- Developing evaluation questions

Objective- Students will learn to gain practice in developing evaluation questions. Learning to ask good questions is essential to good practice evaluation.

For writing and reflection- Read the case example on page 321 of your text. This case example is of a treatment group. Develop three questions that you would want to have answered in order to measure the impact of the group.

Question 1

Question 2

Question 3

For writing and reflection

1. Do your evaluation questions measure only one variable at a time? Questions that seek to measure more than one variable at a time are problematic.

2. What potential methods might be use to answer each question?

3. What are the advantages and weaknesses of each potential method?

4. Will you be able to answer the questions?

5. What will you potentially learn of the questions are answered well?

6. If you attempt to answer your questions, are their any risks for clients?

Exercise 13.3- Case example: Assessing the context of evaluation

Objective- Students will learn to assess the feasibility and likelihood for successful agency evaluations.

Case example

You are one of fifteen social workers who conduct groups in your foster care agency. Your director, Carlos, asked you to evaluate the effectiveness of the group component of the program. There are several types of groups that your agency provides. The most popular are support groups for foster parents. In these groups, workers help foster parents learn to cope with their challenges. Your agency provides services to the Latino and the South East Asian community. The majority of the foster parents in your program are white. About half of the case workers do not have formal education in social work, but are members of these communities. The other half are white social workers with BSW and MSW degrees.

Carlos informed you that you would be given a release of ten percent of your time to conduct the evaluation. He said that you would have a total budget of five hundred dollars. Carlos made it clear that he chose you for the job since your enthusiasm, openness to growth, and education would be helpful in conducting an evaluation. As you have only been with the agency for a year, he let you in on some of the history of evaluations at the agency. Five years ago, researchers from a local university were contracted to provide an evaluation of the program. Many of the workers were resistant to the evaluation process. The researchers implemented many changes in the documentation process specifically for the evaluation. Workers felt unduly burdened by the changes. Each week, group leaders were required to complete an assessment of all their clients' growth towards their five most important goals. The researchers became frustrated with the workers' non compliance. When they finished the evaluation, they provided a report that most of the workers found offensive. Some of the workers said that the researchers did not pay attention to cultural issues, citing their heavy handed criticisms of the late start to some groups. Carlos wants you to figure out a way of conducting an evaluation that does not upset the staff He is under pressure from upper administration to prove the impact of services. He does say, however, that you will have his total support in completing the project. He asks you to think about the project and come back to him in a couple of days to discuss your involvement.

For writing and reflection- Use these questions to help you decide what you would want to discuss with Carlos about taking on the project.

1. What are the most significant barriers to this project?

2. . How will you discuss the project with your coworkers?

3. How might clients be involved in the process?

4. What skills can you use to help the other workers become invested in the evaluation project?

5. What might some of the workers reluctance and resistance be?

6. How can you deal with the resistance in a way that will help the evaluation process?

7. What are some methods for making the evaluation process as unobtrusive as possible?

8. How might this project impact clients?

9. Are the resources provided (time and money) sufficient for completing the project? If not, how might you obtain these resources?

10. After reviewing your answers to the preceding questions, develop a plan of action.

CHAPTER FOURTEEN-ENDING THE GROUP'S WORK

Exercise 14.1- Ending group meetings

Objective-To help students become more aware of the issues involved in ending a session.

For writing and reflection- After reviewing pages 435 and 436 in your text, answer the following questions.

1. What are the most important issues pertaining to ending a group meeting?

2. How would ending a task group and a treatment group differ?

3. What issues must you pay attention to when ending groups with different ethnic and racial populations?

4. What skills do you need to improve to be more effective at ending group meetings?

Exercise 14.2- Worker feelings regarding termination

Objective-Students will develop insight as to how they respond to ending, termination, and loss.

Workers must be able to help members through the often difficult termination period of a group. For many clients, group experiences have been profoundly meaningful sources of change and growth. For some, group membership may have represented the first time they have felt truly accepted and validated in their lives. Therefore, being able to handle the emotional reactions of group members is crucial for group leaders. Also, termination reminds people of generalized losses in their lives and can trigger unresolved grief reactions.

Group leaders often have issues of their own around the topic of termination. We all bring experiences from our pasts into the group. Group workers are not immune. Group workers must be conscious of how their own emotional and behavioral styles concerning endings impact group members.

For writing and reflection

1. What is the hardest part about endings for you?

2. How do you typically deal with endings?

3. What about your style of dealing with endings do you think is valuable to keep?

4. Are there any parts of your style pertaining to dealing with termination that you would like to change? What would you change? If so, what are they?

5. How might you go about changing these behaviors?

For continued writing and reflection-The following questions pertain to more general considerations about endings and terminations of group. Make sure to review the chapter in your text before completing these questions.

1. What are the most important considerations in terminating a treatment group?

2. What are some ways of helping members to continue their interpersonal growth and learning after the group has ended?

3. What negative consequences might there be if members do not fully process the ending of the group?

4. How would you handle a group member who has been dropping hints during the preceding few sessions that the ending of the group represents a painful experience, but expresses only positive feelings during the closing session?

5. The treatment group you are conducting is holding a follow up session a couple of months after the end of treatment. What sort of planning should be considered for this group?

Exercise 14.3- Ending group meetings case example

Charles is a clinical social worker at an inpatient drug and alcohol treatment center in a Veterans Hospital. For the past twenty weeks, he has conducted a therapy group with eight veterans. The purpose of the group has been to help the men come to grips with the issues that have led to their use of drugs and alcohol. A key premise of the program is to help men work through the social issues that act as triggers to substance use. The group was very mixed in terms of ages and ethnicity. Two of the men were African American, one was Asian, another was half Latino. Three of the men were gulf war veterans, the rest were older Vietnam vets. It was the first time in treatment for two of the men, the others each had been in treatment at least once before.

The start of the group was very difficult. Group members were resistant or reluctant for different reasons. Many of the men had learned in their lives and in the service that "real men" did not discuss their feeling in front of others, and that to do so was a sign of weakness. A young man of Chinese descent learned from his family of origin and culture that to discuss one's problems was to bring shame onto the family. During the early sessions of the group, Charles did a good job of addressing these issues. He recognized that some of these men may not always comfortable talking about their feelings, and at times would prefer to be action oriented. Charles conducted exercises that focused on behavioral change, and validated discussion of affect when members of the group brought them up. Over time, the men became comfortable with each other and began to discuss their feelings as well as their thoughts and behaviors in more intimate detail. Three weeks before the group was to end, Charles brought up the topic of termination. He told the group that it was typical for people to have a hard time when things end, especially with experiences where people got to know each other well. Realizing that the men may be reluctant to explore these difficult feeling on a group level, he asked them to spend a few minutes writing about how they typically leave situations. He told the group that it was his pattern to minimize endings, stating that he would tell casually tell others that he would "see them later." He let them know that he had to work hard at not minimizing endings, since this was his natural pattern. After the group members wrote for about ten minutes, he asked the men to share what they wrote in dyads. After the men talked in their dyads, he asked the group members to share with the group as a whole what they discussed, if they were comfortable.

For writing and reflection

1. What skills did the group leader exhibit?

2. Do you agree with the timing of the leaders discussion of endings? Write about your reasons for agreeing or disagreeing.

3. What was the most effective intervention?

4. What would you have done differently?

5. What would be some intervention options during the last half of these meeting?

6. How would you address the issue of endings during the next two sessions?

References

Furman, R. (2002). <u>Culturally sensitive social work practice with Latinos</u>. Doctoral dissertation. New York: Yeshiva University.

Jacobs, E. E., Masson, R. L., & Harvill, R. L. (2001). <u>Group counseling: Strategies and skills</u>. Pacific Grove, CA: Brooks/Cole.

NOTES

NOTES